HANDY LITTLE GUIDE

Novenas

Allison Gingras

Our Sunday Visitor
Huntington, Indiana

Nihil Obstat
Msgr. Michael Heintz, Ph.D.
Censor Librorum

Imprimatur
✠ Kevin C. Rhoades
Bishop of Fort Wayne-South Bend
December 5, 2023

The *Nihil Obstat* and *Imprimatur* are official declarations that a book is free from doctrinal or moral error. It is not implied that those who have granted the *Nihil Obstat* and *Imprimatur* agree with the contents, opinions, or statements expressed.

Our Sunday Visitor Publishing Division
Our Sunday Visitor, Inc., 200 Noll Plaza, Huntington, IN. 46750; www
.osv.com; 1-800-348-244

ISBN: 978-1-63966-180-0
RELIGION—Christian Living—Prayer.
RELIGION—Christian Living—Spiritual Growth.
RELIGION—Christianity—Catholic.

eISBN: 978-1-63966-181-7
LCCN: 2023951527

Cover and interior design: Amanda Falk
Cover and interior art: AdobeStock

PRINTED IN THE UNITED STATES OF AMERICA

Contents

1. Discovering Novenas   5

2. History of the Novena   9

3. Biblical Connections   13

4. The Novena Prayer Mindset   17

5. Novena Fundamentals   22

6. Indulge Me for a Minute   28

7. Flexible and Joyful   32

8. Remembering to Pray   35

9. What Novena Should I Pray?   41

10. Gather Your Saint Posse   43

11. Make Friends with
the Poor Souls   47

12. Novenas to Add
to Your Repertoire   50

13. Novenas with
Extra-Special Blessings   58

14. Miracles Happen   63

1
Discovering Novenas

In 1984, I was a freshman in high school and not exactly navigating life with flying colors. While visiting my best friend, her mother, Andrea, noticing my distress one day, handed me a one-by-two-inch plastic-coated card. On one side was a young nun holding roses, and on the other a prayer to be recited for five days for a particular intention. Andrea explained that this was St. Thérèse of Lisieux, who died at twenty-three years of age, and promised: "After my death, I will let fall a shower of roses. I will spend my heaven doing good upon earth. I will raise up a mighty host of little saints."

A few weeks later, in the throes of teenage angst, I dug out the card and prayed my very first novena. My intentions were simple — a car, a job, and a boyfriend — all typical teenage priorities. After completing the steps explained on the little card, I waited for my rose. Later that day, while attempting to hit a wayward birdie in badminton, I landed in a rosebush and banged my knee against a hidden concrete block. This first little adventure in prayer sent me to the emergency room and back to my friend's mom for further instruction on prayer.

Andrea, knowing I was fine, chuckled at my first encounter with Saint Thérèse. She reminded me that prayer is not a vending machine; you don't put in your prayer "coins" and get to pull the lever for whatever you want. Andrea and, of course, God knew my heart; they both recognized my naive stance on prayer. This way of thinking can clearly be dangerous — just ask my bruised knee and ego.

Prayer, at its core, is a conversation with God. It is as Saint Thérèse said: "For me, prayer is a surge of the heart; it is a simple look turned toward heaven, it is a cry of recognition and of love, embracing both trial and joy." While some prayers are answered as we will, every prayer is, more importantly, answered according to God's perfect will. In Matthew's Gospel, we are encouraged to come to God with prayer, as Jesus teaches us, "Ask, and it will be given you; seek, and you will find; knock, and it will be opened to you" (7:7). Jesus would not instruct us to do so if prayer were not efficacious and meritorious.

The effect of that first foray into praying a novena? I learned prayer's most significant outcome: the change it brought about in me. Andrea helped me come to a deeper understanding of what prayer is. I found profound peace in my situation, developing new patience in waiting out God's plan instead of trying to force mine. Fast-forward: By the end of that year, I had not one but three part-time jobs; my father surprised me with a car; and the new boyfriend has become my husband of over thirty years.

The Saint Thérèse novena became one of my go-to prayers, especially before I travel. One of my favorite stories of Thérèse's intercession happened as I tried to catch a connecting flight from Burbank, California. My flight was canceled, and the airport offered no further flights to Denver that day. The gate attendant handed me a taxi voucher and sent me outside to find a ride to LAX during rush hour, with my next flight boarding in an hour. Dejected, I exited the terminal, looked at the very long line of cabs, and prayed (begged) for Thérèse's assistance. At that moment, a cab driver waved me over; I handed him my luggage and slumped into the backseat, worried but hopeful. An audible laugh tumbled from my lips as I eyed the full-sized box of tissues on the seat — covered in images of red roses. I made the flight and have never traveled since without first finding that forty-year-old prayer card and seeking the peace of a little heavenly assistance.

2
History of the Novena

The Catholic Church essentially began with a novena. For the nine days after the Lord's ascension, the Blessed Mother, along with the Twelve Apostles, remained in the Upper Room in prayer. Their faithful nine days of prayer is considered both the first and oldest novena, and one directly requested by Jesus, as he instructed the apostles to pray in anticipation of the Holy Spirit. The Acts of the Apostles recounts: "Then they returned to Jerusalem from the mount called Olivet, which is near Jerusalem, a sabbath day's journey away; and when they had entered, they went up to the upper room, where they were staying" (1:12–13). And, "all these with one accord devoted themselves to prayer, together with the women and Mary the mother of Jesus, and with his brethren" (1:14). That first novena culminated in the dramatic arrival of the Holy Spirit at Pentecost.

It is fitting that the Church would recognize an invoking of the Holy Spirit as its first novena prayer, as it is through the Spirit all prayer should commence. The *Directory on Popular Piety and the Liturgy*, from the Vatican's Congregation for Divine Worship and the Discipline of the Sacraments, tells us, "The faithful are well used to invoking the Holy Spirit especially when initiating new undertakings or works or in times of particular difficulties" (no. 156).

The Pray More Novenas website, on its blog portion of its site, shares a pre-Christian history of the practice of nine days of prayer for a specific purpose, citing that it

> may have developed more widely in the Church by 'baptizing' a similar ancient Roman practice. The Romans would often celebrate nine

days of prayer to avert a predicted tragedy, offer thanksgiving, or to mourn someone's death. Similarly, the early Christians did have a custom of offering nine days of Masses and prayers for a newly departed soul. In addition to the novena of mourning, different types of novenas began to emerge over time.

We see the popularity of novenas emerge during the papacy of Pope Pius IX (r. 1846–78) with the recommendations of the novena to the Holy Trinity and the Immaculate Conception Novena by granting indulgences (more on that in a bit). Devotions have this unique and beautiful element of being both communal and personal; novenas are no exception. While the early use of novenas leaned more public, as the Church's blessing upon them blossomed so did myriad ways the faithful would practice the devotion.

Fr. William Saunders defines a novena:

A nine-day period of private or public prayer to obtain special graces, to implore special favors, or make special petitions. (Novena is derived from the Latin *novem*, meaning nine.) As the definition suggests, the novena has always had more of a sense of urgency and neediness.*

As happens with the evolution of language, the word *novena* has taken on the meaning of any prayer said for a specific intention over a specific amount of time. As my story with the Saint Thérèse Novena illustrates, since the Upper Room many variations on the length of time for a novena have developed. Whether the novena lasts nine minutes, nine hours, five days, forty days, or fifty-four days, all are valid ways of praying for intercession in your time of need.

---

* https://catholicexchange.com/what-is-a-novena
-what-is-its-origin/

3
Biblical Connections

In the Old Testament, we read the prayer of Queen Esther, uttered when seeking the Lord's help and blessing. The evil Haman had convinced King Ahasuerus, Esther's husband, to issue a decree to destroy the Jews. Esther's uncle, Mordecai, beseeches her to help her people by appearing to the King without being summoned, an act that could end in her quick death:

> And Esther the queen, seized with deathly anxiety, fled to the Lord. ... "And now, assist me, who am all alone, and have no one but you, O Lord, my God. Come to my aid, for I am an orphan. Remember,

O Lord; make yourself known in this time of our affliction, and give me courage. ... And save me from my fear!" On the third day, when she ended her prayer, she took off the garments in which she had worshiped, and clothed herself in splendid attire. Then, majestically adorned, after invoking the aid of the all-seeing God and Savior, she took her two maids with her. (Esther 14—15:2)

Who hasn't had moments of being seized by worry, doubt, or fear? We can turn to the Scriptures and Esther's novena, of sorts, as she prayed and included others, in this case her handmaids, for three days. Esther recognized that the only place to turn, the only one with power over all things — the power to hear the voice of those in despair, to save us from the power of the wicked, and to deliver us from our fears — is God! We communicate with God through prayer, and this devout act of prayer and fasting for multiple days moved his heart, but, more importantly, strengthened Esther's faith, hope, and trust.

No one had more daunting missions than Jesus. Before embarking on these, he would retreat and pray, often for days at a time, such as when he spent forty days in the desert before his public ministry. Jesus prayed and fasted; while fasting is not a requirement in novena prayers, it is, as Jesus models, a powerful practice to add sacrifice and penance to our prayers. More on this later.

In the story of the widow and the judge, Jesus "told them a parable, to the effect that they ought always to pray and not lose heart":

In a certain city there was a judge who neither feared God nor regarded man; and there was a widow in that city who kept coming to him and saying, "Vindicate me against my adversary." For a while he refused; but afterward he said to himself, "Though I neither fear

God nor regard man, yet because this widow bothers me, I will vindicate her, or she will wear me out by her continual coming." And the Lord said, "Hear what the unrighteous judge says. And will not God vindicate his elect, who cry to him day and night? Will he delay long over them? I tell you, he will vindicate them speedily. Nevertheless, when the Son of man comes, will he find faith on earth?" (Luke 18:2–8).

The widow demonstrates how the judge's heart is moved by her persistence, just as our willingness to come to the Lord repeatedly, with the same prayer intention, shows our faith. Pay attention to the judge's words — he will gratify the widow's demands quickly because of her tenacity. If this unjust judge will act this way, out of trying to be done with the woman, how much more will God, out of love, hear and answer the prayers of a faithful, steadfast daughter or son.

4
The Novena Prayer Mindset

Before jumping into the what, when, and how of praying novenas, let's explore more closely a spiritual attitude best suited for this form of prayer.

God Hears Our Prayers

All prayer is good, all have merit, and I guarantee all will have some positive outcome, though most of the merit and grace will be found in what prayer does to the one who prays. He may not change our circumstances, but God will certainly touch and change our hearts. As the *Catechism of the Catholic Church* explains:

Some even stop praying because they think their petition is not heard. Here two questions should be asked: Why do we think our petition has not been heard? How is our prayer heard, how is it "efficacious"? ... Are we asking God for "what is good for us"? Our Father knows what we need before we ask him, but he awaits our petition because the dignity of his children lies in their freedom. We must pray, then, with his Spirit of freedom, to be able truly to know what he wants." (2734–36)

The more time in prayer we spend, the closer to God we grow, which leads to our continual growing in attention, devotion, and love of God, even when not in the midst of a novena: "Draw near to God and he will draw near to you" (Jas 4:8).

What Not to Do

As with all things, the growing popularity of something good can lead to abuses and misconceptions, and novena devotions are no exception. As so wisely explained by the Marian Fathers: "There are no absolute guarantees. Prayer must always be made according to the will of God. Even Christ himself prayed, 'Not my will, Father, but Yours be done.' We pray with trust that God will give us what he knows is best for us."*

The other abuse is believing we can follow certain steps to assure the outcome of our novena prayer — which is, actually, a form of superstition. Other examples include burying a statue of Saint Joseph upside down outside my house when I want it sold or hanging rosary beads outside my window to ensure sunny weather on my wedding day. Other novenas ask petitioners to leave copies of the prayer on church pews or have the prayer and their intentions printed in the lo-

---

*https://www.shrineofdivinemercy.org/what-are-novenas

cal paper (or more recently, online). Even the fifty-four-day Rosary novena I prayed has been referred to as "the never-fail novena" — a misnomer, because God answers prayer according to his loving omnipotence.

As the prophet Isaiah reminds us, the Lord's "thoughts are not your thoughts, / neither are your ways [his] ways" (Is 55:8). The plan God has for our lives is perfect, and we could spend a lifetime contemplating his mind, ways, and thoughts and not make a dent in uncovering their depth. Additionally, at least for me, tremendous solace can be acquired in this famous quote attributed to Saint Teresa of Ávila: "There are more tears shed over answered prayers than over unanswered prayers."

Adding Sacrifice

I am not recommending a forty-day fast from food like Jesus did, or even nine days of that, but we've all experienced denying ourselves one thing or another for the duration of Lent. We also see Jesus counsel the disciples when they fail during their ministry — even when reminding them, "if you have faith as a grain of mustard seed" (Mt 17:21) you can move mountains — that there are situations when we need to recognize "this kind cannot be driven out by anything but prayer and fasting" (Mk 9:29).

As a child, I always gave up candy for all of Lent, which in retrospect was an odd choice because sweets were not something I ate every day. It is far easier to sacrifice an occasional treat than something that is part of our daily routine, such as coffee, television, complaining, or social media scrolling. While these may be more difficult, maybe they will be the very thing to move whatever mountain you face in your life and leave you more open to God.

5
Novena Fundamentals

All prayer should begin with the Sign of the Cross, as it invokes the Triune God — Father, Son, and Holy Spirit. As *The Directory on Popular Piety and the Liturgy* states:

> A Trinitarian orientation is therefore an essential element in popular piety. It should be clear to the faithful that all pious exercises in honor of the Blessed Virgin May, and of the angels and saints have the Father as their final end, from whom all thing come and to whom all things return; the incarnate, dead and resurrected Son is the only mediator (1 Tm 2:5) apart

from whom access to the Father is impossible (cf. Jn 14:6); the Holy Spirit is the only source of grace and sanctification. (158)

Father Mitch Pacwa, SJ, a respected Scripture scholar, recommends three essential elements for the use of novenas:

First, the prayers are specific, which helps us make our needs before God specific without telling God how to answer our prayer.

Second, the prayers include an expression of trust and confidence in God's ability to answer them. "Often we have some doubts, so we pray like the man with the epileptic son," he said. "'Lord, I believe; help my unbelief.' Prayers that rouse our trust in God are aids to the graces of faith and hope."

Third, repeating prayers and repeating them over time is helpful because we often need that length of time to move beyond merely making a request to learning to listen to God as he speaks to us in prayer.

"Getting the answer we seek is only part of the issue," according to Father Pacwa. "It is also essential to see that the length of time to pray the novena induces us to consider more aspects of the importance of receiving the answer."

"We develop our relationship with God, and that is often more lasting than the actual result we see from praying with faith," he says. "The relationship with God himself is essential, and a novena reminds us that the relationship takes time."

In his book *The Church's Most Powerful Novenas,* the late Michael Dubruiel lists three main benefits of praying a novena:

- It helps develop the habit of daily prayer.
- It reinforces a sense that God is our Father and that he loves us.
- It teaches us the benefits of praying with others to God.

Now seems an excellent time to emphasize that imperfect prayer is still valid; our heart, our intentionality, is what matters. If a child tries to put away the laundry, but it's not done perfectly, you're still moved by the attempt, even if it means ironing the clothes for the next week. So it is with God. His heart is moved by our acknowledging that we need him and our persistence in prayer. A novena of any kind builds our relationship with our heavenly friends; persistence in prayer changes us, teaches us how to be holy as God is holy, and grows us spiritually. Even the most imperfect prayer benefits the one who prays.

In fact, if you are holding this book, it is evidence of the most imperfect prayer being answered by God's loving mercy. I did the fifty-four-day Rosary novena, a prayer I received from a wonderful woman in her late eighties who had prayed it most of her life. Sitting in a prayer meeting, which I only attended because it happened to occur during an unexpected visit to a friend, placed me next to this woman. When I shared a difficulty I had been struggling with that year, she reached into her purse and pulled out a tattered little gray-blue book. Its pages were filled with many little pencil marks of dates she had begun and ended her fifty-four-day Rosary novenas over the years.

This generous, sweet woman told me that the most challenging things in her life she had navigated through praying this prayer. It gave her a new understanding of seeking the intercession of our Blessed Mother; of building a beautiful and powerful devotion to the Rosary; and of learning to trust God in every situation, especially the most difficult.

In my own 54-Day Rosary novena, I prayed in anticipation of completing this book; I asked God for the wisdom, focus, and health to write what God wanted and to write it well. My novena was filled with forgotten days. I've prayed the novena prayers separately from the days I prayed the Rosary. A couple of times, I prayed the Rosary twice in one day because I missed it the day before.

But my imperfections didn't matter; what mattered was the fact that I knew that I needed God to complete this task, and that I came to him imperfect and human but faithful.

6
Indulge Me for a Minute

Devotions help us give order and structure to prayer, and they come with blessings and graces. Some offer additional benefits in the form of an indulgence, either plenary (full) or partial. Only one indulgence can be gained each day — the sole exception being the day one dies. That God offers partial forgiveness of our temporal punishment when we fail to meet the conditions of a plenary indulgence illustrates how generous our loving Father is. He offers the mercy of forgiveness, even when we do it imperfectly (all indulgences require us to have a detachment from sin, which can be difficult).

What's an indulgence, anyway? Say you borrow my car, and you have an accident

which is completely your fault. You are re-
morseful for your mistake when you bring
the car back. We're friends, and I recognize
no one is perfect, so, of course, I forgive
you; however, there is still a matter of the
damaged car to be dealt with. You are still
responsible for paying for repairs. Temporal
punishment is the reparation that we owe
God to repair our relationship with him,
even after we have been forgiven our sins
through the Sacrament of Reconciliation.
Receiving an indulgence is like your insur-
ance covering all the damages in full.

Jesus is the grantor and the benefactor
of an indulgence through the gifts he gave
the Church. He steps in and takes all the
liability himself. Our premiums are simply
faith, trust, prayer, and love, already gifted
to us; we merely do our best to cooperate
with them and become the recipients of
grace upon grace. We receive forgiveness
and the cleansing of our souls necessary
for us to enter heaven, as no soul can enter
heaven with any blemish whatsoever. Seems

a fair trade for giving the Lord nine days of my attention, devotion, and love through prayer!

Here's a quick recap on plenary indulgences:

- A plenary indulgence can be gained only once a day. To obtain it, the faithful must, in addition to being in the state of grace;
- have the interior disposition of complete detachment from sin, even venial sin;
- have sacramentally confessed their sins [within several days (about 20) before or after the indulgenced act];
- receive the holy Eucharist (it is certainly better to receive it while participating in Mass, but for the indulgence, only holy Communion is required);

- pray for the intentions of the pope.*

The *Enchiridion of Indulgences* states:

> The condition of praying for the intention of the Sovereign Pontiff is fully satisfied by reciting one Our Father and one Hail Mary; nevertheless, each one is free to recite any other prayer according to his piety and devotion.

---

* See *The Gift of the Indulgence*, Cardinal William Wakefield Baum, major penitentiary, Bishop Luigi De Magistris, titular bishop of Nova Reg, January 29, 2000, vatican.va, 4.

7
Flexible and Joyful

Like many people, you might avoid praying novenas because you worry you won't pray it correctly, that somehow you'll mess it up. Here's a little secret: Like the liturgy and sacraments, which have a "rite" way of proceeding, a novena does not. Unlike the Mass, while devotions have structure, if you miss a step (or a day) they are still valid prayers.

God is our loving Father. Imagine his delight when we come to him, day after day, trusting in his loving kindness and surrendering our needs to his holy and perfect will. Consider a child and their first attempt at coloring, walking, or even eating. Sometimes, these things get messy. Loving parents would not discount their child's attempts nor punish their efforts. Remember, it is never about perfection, but the intentions of one's heart. Prayer, like other pleasures God provides us here on earth, is meant to delight and courage, and, yes, bring us joy. Our prayer brings God joy as well.

A word here about joy, a fruit of the spirit: It is not the same as the emotion or feeling of happiness. Happiness, as they say, is fleeting. Joy in the Lord is our strength, comfort, and consolation. Joy means recognizing that regardless of our circumstances, heaven is possible, present, and offered with great love by God to us. Joy cannot be stolen or darkened by unanswered prayer because true joy comes from being able to bring petitions, praises, and prayers to God in the first place! That he allows such a gift is remarkable. We are blessed to have the ability to talk with God, and we are allowed to interact with all of heaven; the veil between us is so thin that we do not need to wait till we pass to enjoy friendship with our friends in heaven and purgatory.

The answer to every prayer I've ever recited — especially since the first novena when the understanding of God's perfect loving will was opened up to me — has always been peace and an increased strengthening of my faith. Who could ask for a better answer to a prayer?

8
Remembering to Pray

A giant barrier to adopting the practice of praying novenas comes from concern over forgetting to pray each day. With a dismissive attitude that says, "I am so bad at novenas and remembering to pray," many of us miss out on a treasury of devotions. But here's the beauty of prayer to a God who is not bound by our time or earthly limitations! We can pray with the best intentions, to the best of our abilities, and trust him to bless our efforts.

To be sure, having a plan of action for remaining faithful to praying not only shows our genuine desire to accomplish what we set out to do, but also helps ensure we will remember to pray. Here are a few suggestions that have worked very well for me over the years.

Make Time for Prayer

My grandmother once told me that our guardian angels finish our Rosaries. This is still not an excuse to wait until the end of the day to pray as our pillow hits our head, yet sometimes that's just how life goes; it's messy and busy. Kids get sick, deadlines come due, travel can be delayed, the family needs assistance, and holidays arrive.

However, there are enough blessings to put God first, to wake to "coffee with Christ," and to jump-start the day not only with petition but also thanksgiving and praise to Our Lord. When we put God first, he multiplies our time. He helps us to do what it is he has called us to do for that day. Do not delay prayer, and if you do, do not grow discouraged and give up on the novena — pick up where you are and continue to go, knowing that no day needs to be without prayer and that God knows what we need before we even ask.

Inviting Friends to Pray Along

This advice comes directly from the Scriptures:

> For if they fall, one will lift up his fellow; but woe to him who is alone when he falls and has not another to lift him up. Though a man might prevail against one who is alone, two will withstand him. A three-fold cord is not quickly broken. (Ecclesiastes 4:10, 12)

> For where two or three are gathered in my name, there am I in the midst of them. (Matthew 18:20)

There is power in numbers, particularly when those "cords" mentioned in Ecclesiastes remind each other to recite the day's prayers. You don't need to be in the same place to pray; merely agreeing to offer the novena together will be a blessing — both in remembering and in receiving grace.

Set Reminders

Make saying the novena prayer an event or task on your calendar; if you use an electronic calendar, set the pop-up reminder to alert you each day.

Send yourself an email, or use a website or app that will send a reminder email. When I send myself an email reminder (in which I include the prayers), I will immediately resend the email to myself for the next day. You can also schedule your emails to be received at the most opportune time of each day to assure you can pray without postponing until the email is buried deep within the rest of the days' messages!

Set (Many) Alarms

Consider all the places you can set an alarm (phone, AI device, computer, watch, alarm clock) and put them all into action so you don't miss this important appointment.

Use Sacramentals or Visual Reminders

If you're using a prayer card, leave it on your computer, car dashboard, pillow, or bathroom mirror.

Invoking the intercession of a particular saint or the Blessed Mother? Place her image or statue where you can easily see it and be reminded to pray.

Similarly, put a medal of the saint in your pocket and pray throughout the day for assistance. There are also medals for devotions such as the Infant of Prague or the Sacred Heart.

Pray in the Same Place

In the car on your commute or while dropping the kids at school.

In your home, designate a prayer chair or create a prayer corner.

At the kitchen table or counter with your morning (or afternoon) coffee — I call this my daily "coffee with Christ."

After daily Mass.

When you first sit down at your desk to work each morning.

9
What Novena Should I Pray?

The options are truly as endless as the saints in heaven (see next chapter!). You can pray a novena to any saint you choose for any intention your heart desires — for help for yourself or others (or in thanksgiving), including another person, a family, a wider community, a country, or any circumstance upon your heart.

Finding the intention is probably not your struggle, but more likely you might wonder how to find the perfect saint to pair with your intention? Here are a few options, though I guarantee a simple, "Lord, teach me to pray" will bring the answer quickly:

- Ask your priest.
- Invoke the help of Artificial Intelligence (such as Google or Siri). Simply search, "Who is the patron saint of [fill in the blank]?" There is quite literally a saint for everything — they all lived human lives like our own.
- Search for a specific novena. Many saints were well known for their devotions, such as the Efficacious Novena to the Sacred Heart of Jesus, which Padre Pio recited every day for all those who asked for his prayers.

Can't find a specific prayer? Here's your opportunity to either create one or simply share your intention with the saint of your choice and then pray one Our Father, one Hail Mary, and one Glory Be for nine days.

10
Gather Your Saint Posse

Early in my reversion to the Catholic Faith, I recognized I needed help. Beginning with my rose-y experiences with St. Thérèse, I knew the saints were my friends and that I needed to keep them close by. The Blessed Mother, guardian angels, and the holy ones of God — the saints — stand before God, gazing upon his magnificent face and longing for all of us to be there with them one day. The saints, in particular, drew me because they were, like me, imperfect, grace-seeking people who got it wrong most of the time; yet each one found a way, through grace, to reach the goal of eternal life in heaven. Over time, I cobbled together what I affectionately dubbed my

#SaintPosse. Although the core members change through seasons of my life, I invoke this group of heavenly helpers often, especially in my novena devotions.

We read in Scripture that the saints are by our side along our spiritual journey:

> Therefore, since we are surrounded by so great a cloud of witnesses, let us also lay aside every weight, and sin which clings so closely, and let us run with perseverance the race that is set before us. (Hebrews 12:1)

The Council of Trent declared:

> The saints who reign together with Christ offer up their own prayers to God for men. It is good and useful suppliantly to invoke them, and to have recourse to their prayers, aid, and help for obtaining benefits from God, through his Son Jesus Christ our Lord, who alone is our Redeem-

er and Savior. (Session XXV)

The *Catechism of the Catholic Church* adds:

> Being more closely united to Christ, those who dwell in heaven fix the whole Church more firmly in holiness. ... They do not cease to intercede with the Father for us, as they proffer the merits which they acquired on earth through the one mediator between God and men, Christ Jesus. ... So by their fraternal concern is our weakness greatly helped. (956)

God, in his incredible generosity, has not only given us a road map to heaven, but has given us tour guides — experts that know the way. Each one is more than willing to journey along with us, to bring our petitions, our hopes and dreams, and our heart's desires to the Lord, all the while offering us solace, comfort, and encouragement as we navigate surrendering to the will of God. There is nothing we cannot pray for, and there is no lack of patron saints to whom we can turn.

11
Make Friends with the Poor Souls

As Catholics we believe, "All who die in God's friendship, but still imperfectly purified, are indeed assured of their eternal salvation; but after death they undergo purification, so as to achieve the holiness necessary to enter the joy of heaven" (CCC 1030). The Church teaches that after death, these holy souls can no longer earn merit through prayer or good works; therefore, they cannot pray their own way out of purgatory. It is our duty and privilege to be able to assist them through our prayers, good works, and especially the Holy Sacrifice of the Mass. Therefore, the Church has always taught us to pray for the souls in purgatory. While we can do this anytime,

November is dedicated specifically to praying for the dead.

After being a Catholic for over thirty years, when I thought I knew all things Catholic, I was introduced to a magnificent devotion for the faithful departed. A plenary indulgence, applicable only to the souls in purgatory, may be gained from November 1 to November 8 by devoutly visiting a cemetery and praying for the dead.

Fascinated by this important spiritual work of mercy, I pushed past my uncomfortable feelings around cemeteries, rounded up my family, and made daily pilgrimages during the first week of November to local cemeteries to pray for the dead. It was incredibly moving to walk among the graves, reading names of the people we knew and those we did not know, and to pray for people who died long before our lifetimes or a few whose loss was still fresh on our hearts.

The grace of offering this November novena of prayer for souls changed my faith life forever. My once-gripping fear of death was replaced with overwhelming compassion for these precious souls and compels me to this day to pray daily for the dead. This devotion, according to many saintly accounts, comes with a sweet side benefit of heavenly intercessions from grateful souls. Which of us can't use extra prayer and intercession support for our family?

When we make these pilgrimages of prayer to help our friends and even strangers in purgatory, we are in good company of many saints who also shared a commitment to this devotion. St. Josemaría Escrivá had much to say about having a special friendship with the holy souls, including: "Out of charity, out of justice, and out of excusable selfishness — they have such power with God! — remember them often in your sacrifices and in your prayers. May you be able to say when you speak of them, 'My good friends the souls in purgatory'" (*The Way*, 571).

12
Novenas to Add to Your Repertoire

Is your need immediate, and you can't wait nine days to finish a prayer? How about St. Teresa of Calcutta's "Flying," or "Emergency," Novena? This novena consists of nine Memorare prayers said all in a row:

> Remember, O most gracious Virgin Mary, that never was it known that anyone who fled to your protection, implored your help, or sought your intercession was left unaided. Inspired by this confidence, I fly unto you, O Virgin of virgins, my mother; to you do I come, before you I stand, sinful and sorrowful. O

Mother of the Word Incarnate, despise not my petitions, but in your mercy hear and answer me. Amen.

Mother Teresa would always add a tenth in thanksgiving, knowing our Blessed Mother never fails to help her children. Even if the answer was not as she expected, she knew Mary heard and brought her petition and brought it to Jesus.

During the Year of Saint Joseph (2021), I also learned there is a Memorare prayer to him, as well. Here is one version:

Remember, most pure spouse of the Virgin Mary, Saint Joseph, our beloved patron, never was it known that anyone invoked your protection and sought your aid without being comforted. Inspired with this confidence, I come to you and commend myself to you. Do not despise my petition, dear foster father of our Redeemer, but accept them graciously and pray for me to your adopted son, Our Lord. Amen.

What could be more effective than coming to Jesus through the two people not only entrusted with his well-being, in his most vulnerable state, but whom we know loved deeply?

Perhaps you have a little more time to bring your petition or prayer to the Lord, but maybe you're not able to wait a full nine days. How about a nine-hour novena? Two of my favorites are the nine-hour novenas to the Infant of Prague and the Efficacious Novena to the Sacred Heart of Jesus, which you can find online, but any prayer can be turned into a nine-hour novena. Recite the novena prayers once an hour (it doesn't have to be on the top of the hour each time, just within that hour) for nine consecutive hours. To help me remember to pray, I usually set a timer on my watch, phone, or my AI device.

Perhaps you have a little bit more time,

but nine days still seems like a long time to receive a response to your prayers. You could turn to my favorite five-day novena, to St Thérèse of Lisieux, which should be prayed before 11:00 a.m. each day (no reason is given for this caveat, it is just how it was developed so many years ago):

> St. Thérèse, the Little Flower, please pick me a rose from the heavenly garden and send it to me with a message of love. Ask God to grant me the favor I thee implore (mention petition here) and tell him I will love him each day more and more. Amen.

Pray the prayer, along with the Lord's Prayer (Our Father), Hail Mary, and Glory Be five times each. Prayers are to be recited on five successive days. On the fifth day, recite the Our Father, Hail Mary, and Glory Be, an additional five times.

As you may know, St. Thérèse is known

for sending a sign in the form of a rose to the petitioner that their prayer has been heard and presented to the Lord. A word of caution — the rose sign does not necessarily mean God's answer will be according to your plan, but instead comes as an assurance she has presented them to the Lord.

Our Lady Undoer of Knots prayer and novena, made more widely known by Pope Francis — too long to include here — can be said with or without a Rosary. Since the Rosary comes with promises and graces galore, I do try to complete the Rosary version. The Rosary, for me, is an act of waging war against all the obstacles that fight to keep me from the peace Jesus has for me as I await his answer or the resolution of a situation or circumstance. Regardless of which novena you choose or the timeline in which you pray, be assured the Lord loves that you are using this invaluable gift.

In fact, when unsure what to pray, which novena to follow, or who in heaven to seek assistance from, I personally revert to the one who God himself chose to be the mother of his beloved Son. She is the perfect adorer of the Trinity — Daughter of the Father, Spouse of the Spirit, and Blessed Mother of the Son.

One night as I was drifting off to sleep, I asked the Lord a simple question: "Why the Rosary?" The next morning, I woke contemplating several aspects of the Rosary I'd never considered before. For instance, if you pray the Rosary daily, every day you would:

- Renew your baptismal promises, bless yourself, and set up a hedge of protection against the snares of the devil — just to name a few benefits of blessing oneself. (Sign of the Cross)
- Profess your faith, reminding yourself of what you believe as a Catholic. (Apostles' Creed)
- Ask for an increase in the virtues of faith, hope, and love

(the traditional intentions for
the three introductory Hail
Marys)

• Pray with the very prayer Jesus
himself gave us. (Our Father)

• Invoke the assistance and intercession of the Mother of
God. (ten Hail Marys)

• Culminate each decade of
prayer with praise and gratitude to the Blessed Trinity.
(Glory Be)

• Meditate and grow in understanding of the life of Christ.
(Mysteries of the Rosary)

And, honestly, that is just the tip of the Rosary iceberg. The founder of Family Rosary
(Holy Cross Family Ministries), Father Pat-
rick Peyton, C.S.C., declared Venerable on
December 28, 2017, once said:

I fight for the Rosary not as a fa-
natic or a lunatic, but with the

knowledge that if I have Mary's hand knocking with mine, if I have her eyes searching with mine, then the door will open, and we will find what we need. God cannot take that lightly. And she would not be human if she did not help us when we ask.

If I am going to ask, seek, and knock, as Jesus encourages me to do in the Gospels (see Mt 7:7), who better to invoke to approach that heavenly door, than Mary?

13
Novenas with Extra-Special Blessings

The *Enchiridion of Indulgences* (a Vatican book containing essential information on prayer) notes, "A partial indulgence is granted to the faithful who devoutly take part in the pious exercise of a public novena before the feast of Christmas or Pentecost or the Immaculate Conception of the Blessed Virgin Mary." In addition to participating in public novenas through our parish or a Catholic organization, we can also pray private novenas during these seasons.

Leading Up to Christmas

Tradition holds that whoever recites the Saint Andrew/Christmas novena prayer fifteen times each day from the feast of St. Andrew on November 30 until Christmas Eve will obtain the favor requested. My husband and I have prayed this novena together for more than ten years; we have not received every favor we've asked for, but the time spent together in prayer, especially during that hectic season, has been the best gift God could give us:

> Hail and blessed be the hour and moment in which the Son of God was born of the most pure Virgin Mary, at midnight, in Bethlehem, in the piercing cold. In that hour vouchsafe, I beseech Thee, O my God, to hear my prayer and grant my desires, through the merits of our Savior, Jesus Christ, and of his blessed Mother. Amen.

Leading Up to Pentecost

Novenas to the Holy Spirit take their inspiration from the apostles' nine days of prayer between the Ascension and Pentecost. When he called the Second Vatican Council, Pope John XXIII asked the whole Church to join him in a novena to the Holy Spirit for the inspiration of the council. This novena begins on the day after the solemnity of the Ascension, Friday of the Sixth Week of Easter, even if the solemnity is transferred to the Seventh Sunday of Easter.

Leading Up to the Immaculate Conception

There are specific novenas for the Immaculate Conception, but another idea would be the thirty-three days of prayer involved in Consecration to Jesus through Mary, concluding on the feast of the Immaculate Conception (December 8). You can do the reading and the prayer with or without making the consecration. In addition to St. Louis de Montfort's original consecration, there are many other books and resources now available.

Seeking God's Divine Mercy

The Divine Mercy Novena begins on Good Friday and concludes on Divine Mercy Sunday. While the Chaplet of Divine Mercy may be said anytime, the Lord specifically asked that it be recited as a novena, with this incredible promise, as recounted by St. Faustina Kowalsko, "By this Novena (of Chaplets), I will grant every possible grace to souls," and "I desire that during these nine days you bring souls to the fountain of My mercy, that they may draw therefrom strength and refreshment and whatever grace they have need of in the hardships of life, and especially at the hour of death" (Diary, 1209).

At the National Shrine of the Divine Mercy, the chaplet and novena are recited perpetually at three o'clock, the Hour of Great Mercy. My watch has been set to chime at three o'clock for many years, a perpetual novena of sorts which I began after reading these words in Saint Faustina's diary:

As often as you hear the clock strike the third hour, immerse yourself completely in my mercy, adoring and glorifying it; invoke its omnipotence for the whole world, and particularly for poor sinners; for at that moment mercy was opened wide for every soul. In this hour you can obtain everything for yourself and for others for the asking; it was the hour of grace for the whole world — mercy triumphed over justice. (1572)

14
Miracles Happen

At twelve, my daughter, Faith, who is adopted, received an entirely unexpected scoliosis diagnosis. Her doctor found what is known as an S-plus-one curvature in her spine. Faith's back curved like a slithering snake, 50 degrees, then 48 degrees, and ending with another 28-degree curve. Faith was facing the very real (and scary) possibility of spine surgery.

Within a month of the diagnosis, she began wearing a Boston Brace. Wearing the brace for the prescribed eighteen hours a day was painful for both her and us. Our hearts ached as our sweet, amiable child endured hours of discomfort and pain, yet was still unable to reach the level of comfort promised when she began the brace journey. Despite the most valiant efforts, we were unable to get her time in the brace beyond eight to twelve hours. Desperate to reach the level necessary for it to truly help her, we did what any Catholic parent might — we searched for a heavenly helper, a saint who could become her spiritual advocate and intercede in her hour of great need.

My husband discovered St. Gemma Galgani who, like our daughter, was an orphan. Additionally (and quite remarkably), they both also shared a hearing loss and the spine curvature. Faith was born profoundly deaf, while Gemma lost her hearing due to meningitis, the same disease that caused Gemma's spine to curve and would lead to her also sporting a back brace! Wow! Seriously, this is one of the things about the Catholic Faith I love the most — seemingly always being able to find someone to add to our "saint posse" who not only can intercede for us, but can also empathize with our circumstances because they, too, experienced them.

Kevin and I began a novena to St. Gemma Galgani in hopes that Faith's transition to wearing the brace would go much smoother. The first answer came just a few days into the novena. Faith's school physical therapist called to tell me she'd worked at the orthopedic office that not only fitted Faith with her Boston Brace, but that it is the office where the brace originated. She would be able to help Faith with her brace needs at school (a huge concern weighing on our hearts), adding that she was so familiar with the braces she could "put them on in her sleep." I had to hold back tears as relief washed over me.

The next miraculous intercession, and most dramatic, came less than a year later. Faith received an unexpected and remarkable reduction of her two major curves.

The Boston Brace is meant to hold the curve, to keep it from progressing. Although there are a few reported cases of improvement, this is not the norm. Surgery, for now, is off the table. As the physical therapist said: "So happy Faith beat the odds." We, of course, were quick to credit the incredible power of prayer, along with the medical intervention, which brought about what we consider to be a modern-day miracle.

We have learned from this astounding experience and no longer limit our novena intentions. We pray our novenas with gratitude, faith, and trust — allowing God to be God. We, like Bl. Solanus Casey, "Thank God ahead of time," for whatever the outcome will be. I entreat you to never fear coming to God with a hopeful heart, while also remaining open to accepting his answers. Believe, as I do with all my heart, that God has good reason for offering the Church and his children the incredible gift of novenas.

About the Author

Allison Gingras is the founder of www .ReconciledToYou.com, where she shares the love of Jesus and her Catholic faith with relational stories, laughter, and authentic honesty through the everyday, ordinary occurrences of life.

Allison is a Catholic social media and digital specialist for Family Rosary, Catholic Mom, and the Diocese of Fall River. Gingras developed the Stay Connected Journals for Women series, including her volumes *The Gift of Invitation: 7 Ways Jesus Invites You to a Life of Grace* and *Seeking Peace: A Spiritual Journey from Worry to Trust*, and a new volume coming in 2025 from OSV.

The story of her daughter's adoption was shared in *Encountering Signs of Faith: My*

Unexpected Journey with Sacramentals, the Saints, and the Abundant Grace of God (Ave Maria Press). She has also contributed to numerous books, including *Our Friend Faustina* (Marian Press); the CPA award-winning *The Ave Prayer Book for Catholic Mothers* and *Called by Name Daily Devotional for Catholic Women*; and *Living the Word Catholic Women's Bible.*

She hosts a podcast called *A Seeking Heart with Allison Gingras* and is cohost of the *Catholic Momcast* with Lisa Hendey and Maria Johnson. She is joyfully living out her vocation of a deacon's wife and the mother of three.

You might also like:

The Handy Little Guide to the Liturgy of the Hours

By Barb Szyszkiewicz

The Liturgy of the Hours sanctifies each day with prayer, by following a daily rhythm throughout the liturgical year. If you love praying with Sacred Scripture and you appreciate structure, the Liturgy of the Hours is a perfect fit. It's not a practice you'll pick up overnight - but this guide is exactly what you need to begin.

This is your easy-to-read, down-to-earth introduction to the daily prayer of the Church. Wife, mom, and Secular Franciscan Barb Szyszkiewicz helps you understand and practice this beautiful devotion.

You might also like:

The Handy Little Guide to Adoration

By Michelle Jones Schroeder

In this brief, easy-to-read booklet, you will learn the life-changing benefits of Eucharistic adoration.

You will not only explore the nuts and bolts of Eucharistic adoration but also discover great reasons and times to enter into the presence of Jesus in the Eucharist.

You might also like:

The Handy Little Guide to Spiritual Communion

By Michael R. Heinlein

There is a lot of information online about the practice of spiritual communion, not all of which you might find helpful. So you might be wondering: Is spiritual communion just something between me and Jesus? Is spiritual communion of no value if I can't receive the Eucharist? Is spiritual communion "just" a private prayer or devotion? (It's none of those things.)

Sometimes we may be unable to attend Mass or receive the Eucharist. That's why it's important for Catholics to understand and practice spiritual communion. Gain clarity, comfort, and encouragement in this brief booklet.

Available at
OSVCatholicBookstore.com
or wherever books are sold

You might also like:

The Handy Little Guide to Prayer

By Barb Szyszkiewicz

God knows what's on our minds and in our hearts, but we still need to verbalize our innermost thoughts, feelings, and intentions. That's prayer.

In this easy-to-read, down-to-earth introduction to conversation with God, you'll discover, or rediscover, what you need to be able to "pray without ceasing." Author, mom, wife, and Secular Franciscan Barb Szyszkiewicz helps you strengthen your connection to God through prayer.

Available at
OSVCatholicBookstore.com
or wherever books are sold